# Old Dufftown, Glenrinnes and the Cabrach

Douglas G. Lockhart

Text © Douglas G. Lockhart, 2016.
First published in the United Kingdom, 2016,
by Stenlake Publishing Ltd.
54-58 Mill Square, Catrine,
Ayrshire, KA5 6RD

01290 551122
www.stenlake.co.uk

ISBN 9781840337563

Printed by
P2D Books,
1 Newlands Rd,
Westoning, Bedford,
MK45 5LD

**The publishers regret that they cannot supply copies of any pictures featured in this book.**

# Acknowledgements

I would like to thank the staffs of Aberdeen City Libraries; Aberdeenshire Libraries, Oldmeldrum and Macduff; Aberdeen City and Aberdeenshire Archives, Old Aberdeen; Special Collections, University of Aberdeen; National Library of Scotland, Edinburgh; National Records of Scotland, Edinburgh; Moray Local Heritage Centre, Elgin and Carnegie Library, Ayr and Mr J.R. Ingleby, Blairmore for their help with my enquiries. I am grateful to Dufftown Golf Club (Peter Duncan and Sharon Coull), Geoff Marston, Neil Sheed and Eric Simpson who kindly agreed to the use of their photographs.

*Previous page*: Buchromb Estate was a small property situated on the west bank of the River Fiddich about three miles north of Dufftown. The mansion house was built in 1873 and was regarded as one of the finest in the district. It contained four public rooms, nine bedrooms and dressing rooms and a billiard room, often an indication that it catered for sporting tenants. They had exclusive shooting rights over 300 acres and a share of the adjacent moor ground. The house was destroyed by a fire in May 1953 which was thought to have been caused by lightning fusing a wire. Neighbours helped rescue furniture and antiques but the fire fighters were hampered by a shortage of water to put out the flames. Shortly afterwards the estate was sold to the Aberdeen-based Craigellachie Estates Ltd and Buchromb House remained uninhabited and was demolished in 1969. A modern bungalow now occupies part of the site.

# Introduction

Dufftown in the former county of Banffshire is situated 600 feet above sea level close to where the Dullan Water meets the River Fiddich. The origins of the town date from 22 January 1817 when an announcement was made in the *Aberdeen Journal* that the Earl of Fife intended to establish new villages near Keith (Fife Keith) and on the 'Lordship of Balveny'. By June the town plan – a crooked arm cross – was ready and a second advertisement by the district factor, John Watt at Mether Cluny, indicated that a start to the new community would be made on 10 June when 'STANCES for HOUSES and YARDS will be given off'. The name Dufftown was typical of the period, reflecting its association with the Duff family, however it was not the only name that was considered for the new town as Balvenytown was another possibility. Dufftown made a very successful start and within a month 50 feus had been taken up and this had doubled by 1820. There were many attractions: three Scotch acres of land were attached to each feu that would provide keep for a cow, building stone was nearby and the site was a route centre with roads leading to Elgin, Keith, Glenrinnes and Tomintoul, and the uplands of the Cabrach bordering Aberdeenshire. The surrounding area possessed more advantages. First, following the Excise Act of 1823 the local spring water could be legally used to make whisky, resulting in the opening of Mortlach distillery soon afterwards. Second, 'the beautiful romantic wild scenery' (John Watt, 1817) encouraged the development of tourism.

Dufftown became more accessible after the arrival of the railway from Keith in 1862 and soon after it became possible to travel via Craigellachie and the Speyside line to Grantown and Aviemore. The town became a burgh and by late Victorian times it had several banks, hotels, four churches, a wool mill and a growing number of distilleries. It also hosted monthly cattle markets and feeing fairs for servants were held three times a year. The population grew steadily from 770 in 1841 to 1624 in 1901. This was large enough to support a wide range of shops and its many small bakers and confectioners were famous for the quality of their products. The local economy also benefited from growing numbers of summer visitors following in the footsteps of Queen Victoria who passed through the town in 1867 on her way to stay at Glenfiddich Lodge in the Cabrach. Fresh air, healthy pursuits such as walks to the many beauty spots around the town and golf attracted visitors who often rented property for several weeks. Early in the twentieth century bowling and tennis were added to the list of sporting activities. Guide books of the period highlight many of the attractions in and around the town and souvenir photographic albums were compiled for the tourist market by local bookseller George Maclennan and by chemist George Robertson. In the 1880s and 1890s Dufftown shared in the whisky boom on Speyside when a number of distilleries, including several that would become household names (Glenfiddich and Balvenie), were built on the outskirts. Construction of new distilleries provided work for the building trades as well as employment. The prosperity of this period was also reflected in the expansion of the town when new streets lined with terraced housing (Macduff Place) and small villas (Albert Place; Tininver Street) were built. Many public buildings such as the masonic lodge, hospital, police station and the new schools in York Street also date from this time.

Victorian and Edwardian Dufftown was also fortunate in having an able administration headed by a succession of committed provosts and the townspeople enjoyed support from various benefactors. Among these was the Duke of Fife (1849–1912) who was much respected by the people. He paid for the installation of the sewage system, the village lands were fairly rented and there was public access to the woodland and river banks on his estates from which developed a range of walking routes that delighted Victorian visitors. Another was George Stephen (1829–1921), later 1st Baron Mount Stephen, who was born in Dufftown and helped finance the construction of the Canadian Pacific Railway. Stephen donated generously towards the construction of the cottage hospital and provided a fund for pensions to retired people in Dufftown.

South and west of the town are extensive areas of upland farming and rough grazing which in the mid-nineteenth century were owned by a small number of landowners. The Fife estates extended from Dufftown into Glenrinnes while the Duke of Richmond and Gordon owned much of the Cabrach. The Duke of Fife strongly supported land reform and sold sections of his extensive landholdings believing that the prosperity of the countryside would be better managed in smaller estates. For example the Glenrinnes Estate was sold in 1892 and the factor's house at Mether Cluny about one and a half miles from Dufftown was remodelled to become Glenrinnes Lodge. In contrast the large sporting estate has long historic roots in the Cabrach and remains the predominant type of land ownership today. Lodges, such as those at Glenfiddich and Blackwater on the Richmond and Gordon estates, were built to accommodate shooting parties and were rented for the season by wealthy businessmen. While remoteness may have attracted sportsmen and tourists, the area has suffered from the limitations imposed by poor communications and severe winter weather. The marginal nature of upland hill farming coupled with the tragic loss of life of so many local men in the First World War fuelled depopulation to such an extent that there are no schools, post offices/shops, regular church services or public transport in the parish today. The population at the most recent census was just 69 compared with 534 in 1911 and, as a result, abandoned houses are a sad and striking feature of the landscape.

Most of the photographs in this book were taken between late Victorian times and the 1930s. With the exception of the former mansion at Buchromb, destroyed by fire in 1953, and Kininvie House which is situated to the north of Dufftown, the photographs have been arranged to provide a walking tour that begins at the railway station and then visits Balvenie Castle. The photographic route follows Balvenie Street to reach the Tower at the crossroads in the centre of Dufftown, then into Church Street, descending past the former Free Church and old schools to Mortlach Church and the Dullan Water. Returning to the Tower, the next area to be explored is Fife Street and the eastern suburbs. The photographs of the surrounding area are divided into three geographical groupings: Drummuir to the east, Glenrinnes to the west and finally the extensive uplands of the Cabrach south of Dufftown.

*Above*: Kininvie House is situated on the east bank of the Fiddich opposite Buchromb. A house has probably existed on this site since the late fifteenth century and is thought to have been extended during the sixteenth century. The house in the photograph, however, is the result of major rebuilding in 1840 by William Robertson (1786–1841), architect of Elgin, for the laird, Archibald Young Leslie. The resulting design gives the impression of being much older than the mid-nineteenth century. His son, George Abercromby Young Leslie, was responsible for developing the gardens and policies. The estate remained in the ownership of the Leslie family until 1944.

The railway from Keith reached Dufftown in 1862 and the following year the line was extended to Speyside. An account of the first day of passenger services can be found in the *Elgin and Morayshire Courier* of 28 February 1862. The first train left at 6.00 a.m. with only a few passengers bound for Aberdeen; however, the main excitement of the day was reserved for the 9.10 a.m. departure: shops were closed and the provost, a band and 100 passengers, 10% of the population, headed for Keith; hundreds more witnessed the event. In time the basic accommodation for passengers at the station drew criticism from the town council, but the railway company remained unmoved and the facilities were never upgraded. The railway served Dufftown for more than a century until the 'Beeching' cuts began to be implemented. The Speyside line closed in 1965 and the line between Elgin and Keith Junction via Dufftown closed to passengers on 6 May 1968. Freight between Keith and Dufftown, continued until 1984 and the line had occasional visits by the Northern Belle excursion train for a further six years. The last excursion which was organized by Grampian Railtours visited the branch on 24 March 1991. British Rail proposed abandoning the line but the Keith & Dufftown Railway Association, which was formed in 1993, took over and its trains now run between Dufftown, Drummuir and Keith Town Station, a distance of eleven miles. The station building, adjacent platform and the house are still there, although the signal box on the platform and the footbridge have been demolished.

Balvenie Castle & Railway Station, Dufftown. A.2476.

This view captures the romance of Speyside and neighbouring areas. The railway network completed in 1863 meant that travel was now possible over wide areas of Moray and Banffshire, and rivers, hills and historic castles were among the attractions on offer. Dufftown was within five miles of Craigellachie Junction where the Morayshire Railway to Elgin and the lines from Keith and Aviemore all converged on one another and was therefore ideally placed to reap the benefits of tourism. The tourist potential of these lines, which opened up vistas that could not be enjoyed from nearby roads, was quickly recognised. The *Banffshire Journal* on 30 June 1863, the day before the line opened, published a guide to the Strathspey Railway with sketches of some of the more interesting landmarks such as Kininvie Castle and the Thomas Telford designed Craigellachie Bridge. Unfortunately, early optimism contrasted sharply with actual passenger numbers. Passengers travelling between Keith and Elgin preferred the direct route between the two towns and Strathspey was thinly populated. The growing numbers of distilleries in the region from the 1890s did generate more traffic for a time and early in the twentieth century the railway company promoted the 'Three Rivers Tours' on its Deeside, Donside and Speyside services.

**2. BALVENIE CASTLE.**
*from the East.*

H·M·Office of Works

Balvenie Castle dates from the thirteenth century and was built for the Comyns, Earls of Buchan. Since the early fourteenth century, when Robert the Bruce expelled the Comyns, the castle has had a succession of owners. Balvenie was originally surrounded on all sides by a wide ditch which was almost certainly built at the same time as the castle. This can still be seen on the south and west sides, while on the north side there is a cultivated terrace probably dating from the seventeenth century. On the east side, where this photograph was taken, the ditch has been filled in by the sixteenth century owners, the Stewarts, Earls of Atholl, who also re-designed the main entrance to the castle.

The castle was last garrisoned by Hanoverian troops in 1746, immediately after the Jacobite Rebellion. In 1722 Balvenie passed into the hands of William Duff, Lord Braco, but he decided to build a new Georgian mansion – New Balvenie Castle – on a site that later was occupied by Balvenie Distillery (page 9). In this view of the courtyard, two circular stair towers can be seen. The courtyard would also have been lined with buildings; however, only the ruins of a former two-storey building can be seen today. Restoration was carried out by the Office of Works in 1929, the same year as New Balvenie Castle across the valley was demolished. The castle is now in the care of Historic Environment Scotland.

This view looks north towards Glenfiddich Distillery, with the railway station close to the centre of the photograph, Balvenie Distillery to the right and Convalmore Distillery in the distance next to the railway line which heads north towards Craigellachie. The beginnings of Glenfiddich Distillery were distinctly low key. The *Banffshire Journal* of 19 April 1887 reported that 'a small distillery is being built by Mr Wm. Grant, Dufftown'. Five years later William Grant and Sons turned their attention to the conversion of New Balvenie Castle which was owned by the Earl of Fife to form part of the new Balvenie Distillery. Convalmore followed in 1894 and was built in just eight months. It was named after its water supply which came from the Conval Hills. It was rebuilt after a fire in 1909, but in contrast to Glenfiddich and Balvenie, both of which continue to thrive, it closed in 1986, at a time when an excess supply of whisky led to the mothballing of a number of distilleries on Speyside. The distillery was purchased by William Grant's and only its warehouses are in use today.

CONVALMORE VALLEY AND BEN AIGIN, DUFFTOWN.

A more recent view of the valley which covers similar ground to page 9 but taken from a slightly different angle with only the reservoir at Balvenie Distillery visible on the right edge of the photograph. In 1969 Glenfiddich Distillery was the first in Scotland to open a visitor centre located in a former malt barn and warehouse which were part of the original distillery buildings. William Grant's was one of the few companies whose distilleries were open to people interested in how whisky was made and in 1969 Glenfiddich and Balvenie welcomed around 1,400 visitors. Their competitors were at first critical and then they too began to offer tours and whisky tasting so that by 1994 forty distilleries welcomed visitors. Glenfiddich has become a world-famous brand and the visitor centre has become a very popular destination which recorded its 2.5 millionth visitor 30 years after it opened.

John Beaton, the son of a ploughman, was born at Steinmanhill near Fyvie, Aberdeenshire, in 1860. His grandfather had a merchant's business in Dufftown. In 1897 Beaton purchased the licensed grocer's at 40 Balvenie Street and the adjacent house where he can be seen along with his wife Isabella Williamson (1871–1966), their sons and daughter Florence. The postcard was posted on 23 November 1904 by Isabella to her sister Margaret, who lived at Loop between Fyvie and Auchterless Station. She hoped to visit after the Martinmas term, traditionally a busy period for shopkeepers when farm servants had money to spend. John Beaton was also a skilled ploughman and up until his death in 1920 he was a tenant of lotted lands at Dufftown. Afterwards the business was run by his widow and her sons, John Alexander (1894–1922) and James Gordon (1899–1993). Since 1969 it has been owned by the McBain family and remains a licensed grocers' that stocks an impressive range of malt whisky.

In August 1894 a county council committee visited Dufftown, researching a site for a new police station and house. After much debate it was decided in December 1895 to purchase land at the junction of York Street and Hill Street from the Fife Estate. The station was estimated to cost £492 and among the contractors were two local men: William Alexander, mason of Louise Street, and John Wilson, slater of Macduff Place. Building was completed in 1897 and the *Dufftown News* noted that it 'presents a most imposing appearance'. The first constable to take up residence was John Taylor (1862–1941) who had moved to Dufftown from Aberlour in June 1896. He was based in Dufftown for five years and his daughter Mary was the first child to be born at the station (17 May 1898). It served the community for just over a hundred years until a review of policing on Speyside saw upgrading of the office at Rothes which became a hub serving the surrounding communities. Today the former police station in Dufftown is a private house and apart from the loss of the light above the entrance door its appearance has changed very little.

DUFFTOWN FOOTBALL CLUB

The history of football in Dufftown is very complicated as there have been many teams and different locations where the game has been played. The origins of local football appears to date from September 1889 with the election of office bearers of Fiddichside Rangers F.C. and in the years that followed there are press reports of a number of matches involving Rangers. This photograph dates from much later and was probably taken at the end of the 1934–35 season which had been a very successful one when Dufftown F.C. won the Moray Junior Cup and were losing finalists in the Connon Cup. In 1936 the photograph was published as a cigarette card by Ardath Tobacco. That year ended on an unhappy note with the club unable to raise a team to compete in the 1936–37 season. The problem was not confined to Dufftown and the *Courant and Courier* on 18 September 1936 blamed the decline of junior football on a lack of public support. In 1947 the four local clubs put their rivalries to one side and agreed to amalgamate and adopt the name Dufftown Football Club, which plays its matches at Westburn Park near the former police station.

Albert Place was completed and pavements laid in 1890 and many of the houses and public buildings were built around this time. On the left closest to the camera is the hall of the St James's Lodge of Freemasons and construction followed a well-established pattern: the foundation stone was laid in 1886, the building was opened the following year, and in 1888 a bazaar was held to wipe off any remaining debts. The large building with the tall roof on the left further down the street is the parish church hall which could hold up to 700 people and opened in April 1894. Built almost entirely by local contractors, the local blue limestone with freestone dressings from Elgin Quarries gave it a distinctive appearance. The hall was officially opened by the Rev. Dr Marshall Lang, Moderator of the Church of Scotland. It became known as the Mortlach Memorial Hall after the Second World War. The period is also remembered for the villas that were built in the new streets. One such example was Brentwood Villa, built for an accountant working in Elgin which was much admired by the correspondent of the *Banffshire Journal* when he visited in December 1890. This attractive house can still be seen today opposite the Masonic Hall.

This school building brought together on one site schools that previously were in separate buildings in Church Street. Two acres of ground at the west end of Macduff Place were purchased from the Fife Estate and at a meeting of the Mortlach School Board in December 1890 it was decided to proceed with a new infant school. Although the infants' school was built about a year later, it was not until 15 April 1902 that the project was completed and, headed by the Boys' Brigade, the pupils marched from their old schools to the new buildings. Dr Thomas Anderson Stewart (1846–1904), Chief Inspector of Schools in Scotland, was on hand to officially open the new schools. He was clearly delighted with what had been achieved, saying 'I have never seen finer school buildings in my life'. The school, which is still in use today, had accommodation for 650 pupils and cost £6,000, part of which was recovered by the immediate sale of the old buildings.

On the left of this photograph of Macduff Place is the former home of John Wilson (1850–1923), slater by trade. The stone inset between the first floor windows reads 'Victoria Buildings 1892' and many of the other properties in this street were also built around this time. Wilson was born at Corsemaul in the parish of Glass about five miles from Dufftown and in his early years he was employed as a farm servant. After serving his apprenticeship he was in business as a slater and cement and fireclay merchant in Dufftown for over 40 years, during which time he also won building contracts in Aberlour, Rothes and Fochabers. This period coincided with the building boom in Dufftown which saw a growing number of whisky distilleries such as Glendullan and Parkmore, as well as public buildings and villas.

This photograph of Balvenie Street was taken from the Square looking north. The importance of Dufftown is illustrated by the number of shops. On the left are those of Lewis Symon (1866–1929), baker; Robert Hendry of Aberlour (1860–1935), butcher; George Spence (1868–1961), clothier; and also several drapers' shops. The buildings fronting the street which abut directly on to the pavement are a characteristic not just of Dufftown but of planned villages throughout the North East. Many of the original frontage buildings were renovated or replaced during the 1880s and 1890s. Since then, only the three-storey building on the left-hand side furthest from the camera has been lost and its replacement now houses the library. The trees in this and other streets were the gift of the Duke of Fife in 1897.

This view covers much the same ground as the photograph on page 17 but with the advantage of having been taken from the Tower in the centre of town. The cross-streets in the foreground, where men are gathered beside the street light are Albert Place (right, page 14) and Macduff Place (left, page 16). The photograph also allows a rare glimpse into the rear of the large burghal plots where a variety of sheds and byres can be seen with access gained through narrow communal lanes at the front of each contiguous feu. The hay stacks are a reminder that part-time farming was an important activity for many households from the earliest days of the town until the 1930s.

The Elgin and District Motor 'Bus Company (The Grey Line) was formed in 1920 and was a pioneer of bus services in Morayshire. It began on the Lossiemouth and Burghead routes and soon faced competition from other bus operators; it responded by expanding its network. Within a few years its buses were serving places such as Portgordon on the Banffshire coast and Speyside with services to Carrbridge, Aviemore, Grantown and Dufftown. The company also developed an extensive programme of summer excursions. During the early 1930s many local operators sold their businesses to Walter Alexander & Sons Ltd, which had services from Aberdeen to Inverness and had become one of the largest firms of its kind in Scotland. The Grey Line was taken over on 15 June 1936 when it had an operating fleet of twelve modern buses such as the Albion in the photograph and over 30 staff. The garage, a former timber merchant's premises, at 27 Greyfriars Street, Elgin, was not included in the sale. Instead James Watson, the company's enterprising garage manager, began Watson's Grey Line Service Station, offering car repairs, car hire and a carrier agency.

It is not often that an Edwardian photograph can be dated so precisely. The time is 12.50 p.m. on Monday 23 September 1907, which was noted in police records by local Constable James Strath who together with a colleague from Gardenstown was on duty in the Square when King Edward VII passed on his way from Tulchan Lodge near Advie, where he had been a shooting guest, to Balmoral. The photograph was taken by George Robertson (1860–1930) whose chemist's shop was conveniently located in the Square. The King had made this journey a year earlier, stopping to ask for directions to the Cabrach road from the manager at Mortlach Distillery and he followed the same route again in 1908. In September 1911 King George V, who shared his father's passion for shooting game at home and on visits abroad, also stayed at Tulchan Lodge and passed through Dufftown heading for Balmoral.

One of Dufftown's older buildings, the Fife Arms Hotel is sandwiched between two former banks. Facing the camera is the Aberdeen Town and County Bank by Mackenzie and McMillan, architects, Aberdeen. On 15 May 1879 the *Inverness Courier* carried an advertisement for tradesmen to tender for contracts for a bank and agent's house. This was completed in 1881 and it has been recently described as the best building in the Square. Unfortunately in November 2005 the Clydesdale Bank announced that it along with nine others in the Eastern Highlands and Moray would close early the following year. This led to an outcry in the local press and the bank made arrangements for customers to access their accounts at local post offices. The building has since been divided into flats. The Fife Arms Hotel is a typical example of a village inn, centrally located, named after the laird's family and dating from the earliest years of the town. An advertisement in the *Aberdeen Journal* in June 1827 by Mrs Elizabeth Collie (c.1788–1843) hoped that she would continue to enjoy 'the liberal patronage bestowed on her late husband'. The third building forms the corner of the Square and Fife Street and it replaced the Commercial Bank building in the early 1930s. Latterly it housed the Royal Bank of Scotland and a solicitor's office. The branch closed on 15 September 2015 and its services were replaced by twice-weekly visits from a mobile bank.

Church Street, as its name suggests, linked the Square with the Parish Church in the Kirktown close to the Dullan Water. Shops can be found in all the streets leading to the crossroads in the Square. The premises on the left, closest to the camera, is that of Robert J. Mair, licensed grocers, and the next shop was owned by Alexander Allan (1870–1938), a native of Forres who purchased the ironmongers' business that had been owned by John Symon until 1896. There were also two hotels here which probably explains the carriage outside the Commercial Hotel which was enlarged in 1890. The building on the left is Provost Symon's Hall which dates from 1879. It has housed a variety of activities over the years, hotel, public hall and restaurant. It was closed and listed for sale by estate agents in Elgin during 2015; however, it was being renovated when visited by this author in March 2016.

In this view can be seen Mortlach Distillery, the oldest distillery in Dufftown, the terminus of the Parkmore and Mortlach sidings and, in the distance, Church Street with the spire of the Free Church just visible. Mortlach was the only distillery in Dufftown for over 60 years until Glenfiddich was founded. In its early years it changed ownership several times, but in 1853 George Cowie (1816–96), an engineer with expertise in railway construction, joined the distillery. He became sole owner in 1867 and Mortlach became a much sought after whisky. His son, Alexander Mitchell Cowie (1861–1940), trained in medicine and with a flair for engineering took over the business when his father's health began to fail. He worked with Charles C. Doig to expand the distillery, install electric lighting in 1898, and it was his idea to link the distillery to the Dufftown–Keith railway line. The construction of the line, which also served Glendullan Distillery, was quite controversial even though it only extended a siding built in 1891 to serve Parkmore lime works. The siding was completed in 1900 on private land; however, it crossed the Huntly road next to Crachie Bridge on a level crossing, which led to friction between the Dufftown Police Commissioners and the railway company. Shunting operations that occasionally blocked the road were a major irritant. The siding to Mortlach closed in 1964 and the remaining part of the line two years later. In 1923 Mortlach Distillery was sold by the Cowie family to John Walker and Sons.

The *Aberdeen Journal* of 23 September 1794 advertised for tradesmen to submit their estimates for a new manse to be built at Mortlach. The resulting rectangular building was expanded into a much larger Neo-Tudor house in 1844 by the Elgin-based architect Thomas Mackenzie. Mackenzie, in partnership with James Matthews, designed a large number of schools, banks, churches and manses throughout north-east Scotland. The manse is now a private house known as Danesfield.

Mortlach Church is one of the oldest in Scotland and the site has great historical significance. It is reputed to have been founded about 556 AD by Moluag, a contemporary of St Columba. Legend suggests it was rebuilt by King Malcolm II after defeating the invading Danes at the Battle of Mortlach in 1010. However, it is more likely that the rectangular appearance of the present building dates from the thirteenth century. The north aisle was added in 1826 to accommodate the increasing population and there have been further extensions since that included alterations to many of the windows. The church was temporarily closed in 1930 and reopened the following year after the interior was refurbished by Dr Alexander Marshall Mackenzie to recreate the internal arrangements that had existed in medieval times. Only the base of the tall gate pillars remain and the gate has been replaced by a smaller gate halfway down the steps leading into the churchyard.

Mortlach Churchyard contains the memorial stones to many individuals who have shaped present-day Dufftown. These include whisky distillers such as William Grant, founder of William Grant and Sons, owners of the Glenfiddich and Balvenie distilleries; James Findlater, who helped establish Mortlach Distillery; and George Cowie, who had a highly successful career as a surveyor, engineer and distiller, and became the first provost of the burgh of Dufftown. Close to the church there is an early nineteenth century watch house, hidden by the trees, while the grid of paths in the lower ground is an extension to the churchyard that dates from August 1899. This photograph was taken before October 1905 as the memorial to Dr James Innes has not yet been erected (see page 27). At the time of writing a guide to the memorial inscriptions by the Moray Burial Ground Research Group is in progress.

*Left*: This stone was erected on a haugh on the banks of the Dullan Water near Mortlach Church, which was incorporated into the churchyard when it was extended. The stone is visible close to the centre of the still sparsely populated new extension (page 26). It is believed to commemorate the victory of King Malcolm II over the Northmen or 'Danes' in 1010 and is now very weathered, making it difficult to interpret the various figures that are carved on it. However, a drawing of both sides of the stone was published as Plate XIV in *Sculptured Stones of Scotland Vol. 1*, Spalding Club, Aberdeen, 1855–56 when it was less eroded than it is today.

*Right*: Dr James Innes (1839–1905) was born at Keithmore, Auchindoun, about two miles from Dufftown and for more than 40 years he was in general practice in the town and surrounding area. When he died the *Northern Scot* described his funeral as 'the largest and most representative ever held in this district … over 1,000 people were present'. Shortly afterwards a working party was appointed to make arrangements for a memorial stone to be erected in his memory. The stone, which is 23 feet in height and designed by James Hutcheson of King Street, Aberdeen, was placed in position in October 1905. It is still a prominent feature of the lower section of Mortlach Churchyard.

This peaceful scene is of the hamlet and parish church situated at the foot of Church Street close to the Dullan Water. In the eighteenth century travellers would have passed this way on the old road to Glenrinnes and Glenlivet. The houses on the left were built on the Old Glebe Land at different times between 1884 and 1902. The scene was photographed from close to the entrance to Dufftown Distillery and its growth has resulted in a number of changes here. The house facing the camera and the cottage with the distinctive dormer windows have been replaced by distillery workers' housing. Another block has been built just beyond the bush on the right and the wall protecting the stream has lost its rustic charm and now has an altogether more functional appearance.

Charles Joseph McPherson's parents (1866–1932) were in the hotel trade in Elgin and latterly his mother, Patience Fowkes, was licensee of the Fife Arms Hotel in Dufftown. He served his apprenticeship with Thurburn and Fleming, solicitors of Elgin, and began business as a solicitor in Dufftown in 1890. Five years later he made plans to build a house at Priestwell overlooking the Kirktown. Charles Macpherson had a busy business and public life: provost between 1905 and 1911; clerk to Mortlach School Board; clerk and treasurer of the Feuars Managers; and, on different occasions, president of both the golf and bowling clubs. His business interests extended to the agency of the Commercial Bank and Chairman of the Directors of P. Mackenzie & Company Distillers Ltd which owned Dufftown–Glenlivet Distillery where he was the manager. He married Elizabeth Symon (1866–1951), daughter of Provost John Symon, in 1896 and their son, Charles Fowkes McPherson (1898–1950), continued many of his father's business and public duties. The distillery was sold to Arthur Bell & Sons Ltd of Perth in 1933 and is currently known as Dufftown Distillery. Following the death of Elizabeth McPherson, Priestwell passed to her daughter Isobel and she sold the house and adjacent property in 1958 to Bell's. Priestwell was demolished about 1965 and the surrounding area is now given over to bonded warehouses.

Pittyvaich Farmhouse is situated on the old road from Glenrinnes just before it descends steeply to Kirktown of Mortlach. It was purchased by John Symon (1836–1908) from the Duke of Fife in 1890. Until then he owned an ironmongery and saddlery business in Conval Street. Symon had an exemplary record of public service that included holding the office of provost and membership of the county council, parish council and the school board. He was one of the four founding directors of the Dufftown–Glenlivet Distillery; another was Charles McPherson who married Symon's daughter, Elizabeth. The house is thought to date from the mid-eighteenth century though parts of it may be older and in 1972 it was scheduled as a category B listed building. It has been unoccupied for more than 30 years and has been on the Buildings at Risk Register though it was in the early stages of renovation when visited by this author in March 2016.

*Below*: Hardhaugh can be found on the opposite bank of the Dullan Water, close to Mortlach Churchyard. The house was built around 1810 and stood close to an old road between the West Highlands and Aberdeen. It was the original inn of Mortlach Parish before Dufftown was planned and it had cellars downstairs where liquor was stored. Today it is partly hidden by a tall hedge at the start of the walk leading up the valley towards the Giant's Chair.

*Right*: The path to the Giant's Chair was opened up to commemorate the Jubilee of Queen Victoria in 1887. After crossing the Dullan Water by the footbridge of the Kirkton to reach Hardhaugh, the path turns right to run alongside the river. Soon Dufftown (formerly Dufftown–Glenlivet) Distillery, which was converted from a mill in 1895–96 by Charles C. Doig, can be seen on the far bank, followed by a weir known locally as 'the intak'. The water for a short distance upstream is tranquil and afterwards the path becomes more undulating and passes the Linen Apron Waterfall. The main attractions are the natural rock features shaped by the power of the Dullan known as the Giant's Chair, which is close to the shelter, and the Giant's Cradle, seen on the left after crossing another footbridge. The path continues and meets a minor road; turn right and within a few minutes walking Pittyvaich at the top of the hill overlooking the Kirktown is reached.

The Tower in the Square is a striking feature. It was opened in 1839 as the gaol and became the council chambers in December 1895. The clock was originally from Banff and is known as 'the clock that hanged Macpherson'. James Macpherson was an outlaw who was eventually captured in Keith in 1700 by a posse organized by Lord Duff of Braco. He was sentenced to hang in Banff; legend has it that on the day of execution a rider with a reprieve was approaching, but to ensure that the hanging went ahead the clock hands were turned forward by fifteen minutes. Funds remained after the celebrations to mark the Diamond Jubilee of Queen Victoria and the committee decided that the clock should be illuminated and new dials fitted. A memorial to the Duke of Fife (1849–1912) is attached to the east side of the Tower and a plaque on the south side commemorates the achievements of George Stephen (Lord Mount Stephen, 1829–1921) in Canada. Shortly after this photograph was taken four lamps, one on each side of the Tower, were donated by George Robertson, chemist. From the late 1920s until about 1970 it was home to a burgh workman; today, it is vacant.

Fife Street was a much favoured location to photograph the Tower and this view highlights another uniform line of houses which incorporate small shops such as that of Robert Nicoll (1847–1917), baker, near the first tree on the right. He was in business for 40 years. Other shops in the vicinity included a saddler's, watchmaker's and ironmonger's. This was the route followed by Queen Victoria when she travelled through Dufftown to visit Glenfiddich Lodge in 1867. She arrived via the street beyond the Tower, Conval Street that descends from Glenrinnes, and after pausing for a moment in the Square her carriage was said to have been driven quickly down Fife Street. After the royal visit Conval Street was renamed Queen Street though it reverted back to its previous name in 1899.

FIFE STREET, DUFFTOWN, FROM CLOCK TOWER. (1)

This photograph of Dufftown was taken about 1950 and demonstrates that little had changed in Fife Street since the turn of the century, apart from new street lighting. Electric lighting replaced the old paraffin lamps in 1937. The tall two-storey building adjacent the truck is the Royal Oak Inn which is a listed building. By the 1950s larger council housing estates were being constructed and evidence of this can be seen in the middle distance on the left of the photograph where several houses in Mount Street, on the edge of the built-up area, are still without their roofs.

Discussions to establish a bowling club gathered momentum in July 1904 when a field near the Stephen Cottage Hospital was acquired from the Fife Estate. Access was from the eastern end of Tininver Street where villas had begun to be built in 1899. The bowling green was formally opened on 4 July 1906, although funds were still needed for a pavilion and tennis courts. These were raised by the tried and tested method of a bazaar which was held at the town hall around six weeks later. This was opened by the Duke of Richmond and Gordon who was well practised in these occasions as Dufftown was the third event he had attended that week. The Square was decorated for the bazaar, which was a great success, and the new pavilion was opened the following year by Provost Charles McPherson. The bowling green is still there but the tennis courts are now a car park. The view of Tininver Street has also changed. The first council housing in Dufftown (1920) and a semi-detached property (1949–50) built by Alexander Stuart, mason, to house two of his workmen are close to the club on the north side of the street.

Dufftown-born George Stephen (later Lord Mount Stephen, 1829–1921) emigrated to Canada at the age of 21 and played a key role in developing the railway network, becoming president of the Canadian Pacific Railway. When he visited Dufftown in September 1888 he was given an enthusiastic welcome in the town and at Glenrinnes Church where almost the whole population turned out to welcome him. He repaid their friendship with a donation towards a new church for Glenrinnes and announced his intention of endowing a cottage hospital in Dufftown. A board of directors was appointed the following February and two months later it appointed contractors for the building work. On 22 June the *Moray and Nairn Express* reported that 'in weather that would vie with the most bright and cloudless Canadian summer … the foundation stone of the Stephen Cottage Hospital was laid amid manifestations of rejoicing …'. The weather was again fine and the town was decorated with flags, bunting and streamers when the Duke of Fife performed the official opening on 5 August 1890. Over the years Lord Mount Stephen provided additional funding for the expansion of health care at the hospital which is still open today.

General views of Dufftown such as this taken from Meg's Widd (Wood) with Parkbeg Hill in the background are a feature of the photographic albums produced by local shop traders George McLennan and George Robertson. The lotted lands in the foreground were rented from the estate and this enabled feuars (house owners) to grow crops such as hay and turnips which provided the keep for a cow. Oats and potatoes were also grown and surplus produce was auctioned at sales of growing crop in late summer. A tenants' committee known as the Feuars' Managers maintained the feu roads (access tracks), oversaw mole catching and cutting tanzy ragwort and thistles. This field system continued until the sale of the last sections of the Fife Estates in 1961. Another feature of this photograph is new housing. Three villas are visible in the middle distance in Louise Street. From left to right are Glenview, 1897 (William Alexander (1860–1950), mason); Helenslea, 1896 (James Watt (1866–1949), ironmonger; named for his wife Helen Duncan); and Benview, 1895 (James Wilson (1856–1927), draper). Helenslea is now Ladoma, renamed by a later owner, John McLeod, after holidaying in Spain. The villas outwardly are much the same today, although they are now surrounded by a large council housing scheme built in the late 1940s and early 1950s.

This photograph taken in 1911 is of James Wilson (1886–1951), only son of James Wilson, draper, Benview, Louise Street (page 37). He served his apprenticeship with his father and succeeded to the business in 1919. In the First World War he was a railway transportation officer in the Gordon Highlanders and retired with the rank of captain. His social and sporting interests were many: left back for Wednesday F.C. (Dufftown), treasurer of Dufftown F.C., bowler and angler. He was involved in the Church, Choral Union, the Plate Glass Association, the Balvenie Lodge of Oddfellows, the Memorial Hall Committee and was a sergeant in the Special Constabulary. James Wilson died at Benview, six and a half years after his sister Elizabeth Ann, who sent this postcard to a friend, and who was also very committed to voluntary activities and helping older members of the community.

*Left*: St Mary R.C. Church dates from 1824–25 and was the work of the Rev. James Kyle who also designed churches at Fochabers and Tombae in Strathavon. This photograph was taken after a programme of improvements in 1912 involving reducing the height of the wall on Fife Street and the construction of a new entrance up a flight of steps to the church door. The wrought-iron gate was gifted by Lord Mount Stephen. It has a Jacobite pattern and the upper section is decorated with a fleur-de-lys and a Gothic cross. A feature of interest in the sanctuary of the church is a painting of Our Lady of the Assumption which came from the former chapel at Clova in Aberdeenshire.

*Right*: Early in 1920 Dr Alexander Marshall Mackenzie, architect of Aberdeen, produced two designs for a war memorial: one that could be built in front of the Tower in the Square and another suited to a small field on Station Road. Both designs were published in the *Northern Scot* on 14 February that year and the War Memorial Committee decided to ask for the views of the closest relatives of those who had been killed in the conflict. The plebiscite favoured the plan for the Station Road site and the foundation stone was laid on 21 April by Princess Arthur of Connaught, Duchess of Fife, on an afternoon of bright sunshine, an occasion reported in much detail three days later in the *Northern Scot*. Seven months later the Duke of Richmond and Gordon unveiled the monument to the 108 men from the Parish of Mortlach who had lost their lives in the First World War. Made from stone from the Kemnay Granite Quarries, the memorial is 24 feet high. A large number of wreaths were laid by relatives of the fallen and the moving ceremony ended with the Dufftown pipe and drum band playing 'Lochaber no more' and the sounding of the 'Last Post' by Alexander Grant, a local coppersmith. Funds still had to be raised to complete the memorial garden that was part of the design and enclose the one-acre site and this was accomplished the following summer when a bazaar was held in the school hall.

Drummuir Castle, four miles east of Dufftown, was designed by Thomas Mackenzie of Elgin for Vice-Admiral Archibald Duff (1773–1858), who served under Nelson and inherited Drummuir Estate in 1836. The work began in 1848 and was completed two years later at a cost of £10,000. Among its many impressive features, best seen when approaching up the curved driveway are grey-stoned turrets, towers and battlements and the carriage portico. The inner hall has a void three storeys high, flanked by arched galleries, rising through the main part of the castle. The castle has remained in family ownership and was opened to the public for the first time in 1988, after several years of restoration work. In 1994 it was leased to whisky distillers Justerini and Brooks Ltd and, more recently, Diageo for conferences and corporate entertaining.

Drummuir Garden Fete, July 1917

Scotland's Red Cross Week was held at the beginning of July 1917 with the aim of raising £100,000 to help treat wounded and disabled servicemen. A garden fete took place on the lawns of Drummuir Castle on the afternoon of 4 July in support of the appeal. It attracted 3,000 people, some of whom had travelled on a special train from Rothiemay and intermediate stations. The sun shone, the gardens looked at their best, and the crowds were entertained by the brass band of the Gordon Highlanders, a sketch by the Keith League of Honour and a fancy dress cycle parade. A tug o' war brought the programme of events to a close. A number of local voluntary organizations had stalls and an impressive £450 was collected for the appeal.

Development of sports facilities and the economic well-being of towns are often closely linked. Prior to the start of the Boer War, Dufftown was growing, there were new distilleries, and the town was attractive to tourists. The *Banffshire Herald* of 14 December 1895 reported that arrangements had been made with Robert Skirving of Glenrinnes Lodge for the lease of 25–30 acres of the farm of Mether Cluny to form a golf course. The nine-hole course was laid out by Archie Simpson from Aberdeen on sloping ground about one and a half miles from town on the north side of the Tomintoul road. A few months later it was ready for play and it was officially opened by the Rev. John Barr Cumming (1855–1928), the first club captain, on Wednesday 6 May 1896. A club competition followed with medals presented to the competitors with the lowest scores – one for ladies and another for men. The club made a promising start with membership passing the 100 mark and two years later the course featured in the *Illustrated Tourists and Visitors Guide to Buckie and District* which had a wider geographical coverage than its title suggests. The club suffered a temporary reverse when the lower part of the course was ploughed for cultivation in February 1918 and golf did not resume until 1921. The first club house can be seen in this photograph taken in 1929.

Golf Club House, Dufftown.

A.2484

A new club house was officially opened on 14 May 1930 by Miss Isabella Cowie (1901–85) of Glenrinnes and Mether Cluny who also played the opening drive on the course. This had been redesigned by George E. Smith, professional at the Moray Golf Club, Lossiemouth, but it was only played over until the outbreak of the Second World War and as post-war economic conditions were discouraging, golf did not return to Dufftown until 1960. Dufftown shared in the golfing boom of the 1980s when the course was extended to eighteen holes and the sale of Glenrinnes Lodge in 1993 provided the club with the opportunity to purchase the 90 acres that it previously leased from the estate. The asking price was raised through loans from members, a fund raising auction and support from the whisky industry. The clubhouse in the photograph was deliberately destroyed in a fire in October 2000 to make way for the current building which was opened the following July by Bob Strachan, the professional at Duff House Royal Golf Club in Banff.

In 1892 the Duke of Fife sold 6,800 acres of his extensive estates in Glenrinnes, including the farm of Mether Cluny that was once the home of the district factor, to Robert Skirving (1854–1935) of Edinburgh and Cobairdy, Aberdeenshire, whom the 1891 census noted was 'living on private means'. Skirving invested heavily in improvements to the estate and among these was Glenrinnes Lodge which was built in 1895 to a design by George Sutherland, architect in Elgin and Banff. The plan combined part of the old farm house at Mether Cluny with a new section to create a mansion with three public rooms, nine bedrooms, servants' quarters and kitchen area. Mether Cluny had now become a sporting estate, but Skirving did not stay long. He married in 1898 and soon after the estate was put up for sale. The purchaser was James Eadie (1827–1904) of Barrow Hall, Derby, who had made his fortune in the brewing industry in Burton-on-Trent.

Water for this roadside well comes from a spring near Benrinnes plantation about half a mile away. The well features the Eadie family crest and an inscription which reads: "Erected by James Eadie, Esquire, of Glenrinnes, D.L., in commemoration of the Coronation of Their Majesties King Edward the Seventh and Queen Alexandra, 9th August, 1902." The water supply was turned on at the official opening by his daughter Jean (1857–1930). In the distance is Ben Rinnes which rises to 2,755 feet which commands views from Sutherland to the Grampians. Around two-thirds of the Glenrinnes Estate (5,000 acres) was moor ground and together with 300 acres of woodland (Benrinnes Wood) was an ideal environment for the game which Victorian sportsmen sought such as grouse, partridges, pheasants, duck, roe-deer and hares. The estate was purchased in 1925 by Dr Alexander Mitchell Cowie (1861–1940) two years after he had sold Mortlach Distillery to John Walker and Sons. The well can still be seen today opposite the junction of the B9009 and an unclassified road signposted: 'Glenrinnes Graveyard'.

The B9009 Dufftown to Tomintoul road climbs steadily up Glenrinnes for a distance of seven miles. Near the summit at the Glack of Breagach there are a number of deserted crofts. Abandonment in areas such as this has many causes, including the marginal farming conditions experienced here, the loss of young people to emigration, and the high proportion of casualties among local soldiers during the First World War.

Crachie Bridge, Dufftown.

Crachie Bridge spans the Dullan Water close to its confluence with the River Fiddich and is used by traffic heading for Huntly and Rhynie. This picturesque scene appeared in Edwardian photographic albums and also featured in the Christmas number of the *Northern Scot* in 1908. The bridge was replaced by another in a similar style in 1949 which explains the date displayed on both parapet walls. The trees and shrubs are now much overgrown and it is impossible to take a picture like this today. The old embankment of the Mortlach Distillery Siding (page 23) runs parallel with the Dullan at this point.

Auchindoun Castle has a stunning windswept location with fine views up Glenfiddich to the Cabrach. The present castle was built c.1470 by John Stewart, Earl of Mar, younger brother of King James III. In the late sixteenth century it was sacked and burned by the Mackintosh clan in retaliation for the murder of the Earl of Moray. The castle suffered again in the eighteenth century when William Duff of Braco took stone to build a Palladian mansion that became known as Balvenie New Castle. The keep is four storeys high with impressively thick rubble walls. There is a large courtyard and tall walls constructed from large blocks of rubble. Surrounding the walls are earthworks that are believed to be those of an Iron Age fort and the large ditches were probably re-occupied by the Picts. The castle is in the care of Historic Environment Scotland and is signposted from the Cabrach road.

The entrance to the Glen at Bridgehaugh is particularly narrow. There is just enough room for the porter's cottage, the road and the stream. The road follows the winding river for several miles with constantly changing vistas and on each side the hills, which are covered in green sward or brown heather, rise abruptly. Some older trees have grown naturally where pockets of soil have allowed them to root successfully and organized conifer plantations occupy the middle slopes. Closer to the lodge there are a number of footpaths that criss-cross the Fiddich on slender wooden bridges that were ideal for a pre-dinner stroll or for ladies to enjoy while their husbands were out shooting.

The Glenfiddich and Blackwater Deer Forests which were owned by the Duke of Richmond and Gordon covered a very large area to the west of the A941, extending from near Balloch to the county boundary with Aberdeenshire. The remote Glenfiddich Lodge dates from the early nineteenth century and it provided accommodation for shooting parties. The *Elgin and Morayshire Courier* in 1862 noted that 'though neat and comfortable … [it] has nothing particularly striking about it. It is situated in one of the deepest recesses of the glen'. Five years later Queen Victoria, dressed in black mourning clothes and accompanied by Princess Louisa, travelled from Balmoral via Glenlivet and Dufftown for a short private visit to Glenfiddich Lodge. She was favourably impressed and described the rooms as well sized and the food 'though very simple, was excellent …'. She left the lodge to have a picnic lunch overlooking Auchindoun Castle and at the end of her stay she retraced her outward route back to Balmoral.

Since it was first built in 1788–89, Blackwater Lodge was redesigned and extended on a number of occasions during the nineteenth century. The lodge, which takes its name from the nearby Black Water, is in a particularly remote location and can be reached by either turning off the access track to Glenfiddich Lodge or from Ardwell on the A941. It appears on John Thomson's 'Map of the northern part of Aberdeen and Banff-Shires' published in 1826 and the *New Statistical Account* (1842) mentions a shooting lodge on the Blackwater Deer Forest owned by the Duke of Richmond and Gordon. The Richmond and Gordon family continued to own land in the Cabrach until the late 1930s, when many of the farms were acquired by the Crown Estate and shortly after the Second World War the lodges, shootings and some farms were bought by Hugh Borthwick-Norton of Southwick Park, Hampshire.

After passing Bridgehaugh at the gates of the private track to Glenfiddich Lodge, the Cabrach road (A941) becomes a stiff climb up to the Glacks of Balloch. Immediately after the tree line has been left behind, the road follows a narrow heather clad pass between two hills known as Meikle Balloch and Little Balloch, where this photograph was taken. Balloch Well, a short distance away, was a favourite lunch stop of King Edward VII when travelling from Speyside to Balmoral. The quiet surroundings usually ensured privacy, although on one occasion a postman happened to be passing on his rounds and he was invited to join the royal party for a drink.

This photograph was taken from the Dufftown–Rhynie road. The tall building is Lesmurdie House which was built in 1905. The estate was bought by Archibald Leslie of Kininvie (1843–1913) in 1911 and the following year he added the rooftop observatory to the house. Today it is completely hidden by trees. The school building near Milltown appears on the first edition of the Ordnance Survey map which was surveyed in 1869. Four years earlier Thomas Robertson (1840–1909), a native of the Cabrach was appointed schoolmaster of the Lower Cabrach, a post which he held until a month before his death. This school continued to serve the Cabrach area until 1979 when it was replaced by a new building. However, by 2007 the school had just two pupils, ten less than in 2001, and Moray Council proposed transferring the remaining pupils to Dufftown, although this did not take effect for a further three years. The 'new' school is now The Acorn, home to Cabrach Community Enterprise. A few yards away the derelict old school buildings await a new use or more likely demolition.

The Richmond Hotel or Grouse Inn at Nether Ardwell is on the main road between Dufftown and Rhynie. The *First Statistical Account* published in 1796 notes that there was no inn or hotel in Cabrach Parish. The building at the time was a merchant's shop and conversion is thought to have occurred about ten years later. In the mid-nineteenth century, the Grouse Inn, as it was known then, became a popular fishing retreat and attracted merchants from Aberdeen and professional men sometimes from further afield. Considering it is in such an out of the way location the licence has been held by members of only two families since the mid-1870s. James Watt, a farmer took over the licence in 1876 and in 1896 it became known as the Richmond Hotel possibly because the Duke often lunched there and members of his family occasionally stayed. The inn was a favourite meeting place among local lads and a popular venue when events such as stock sales, the Huntly and Dufftown holidays, the Ardwell Picnic and Games and the Cabrach Christmas Tree took place. James Watt was succeeded by his son John in 1912 and only when his widow required surgery in 1938 did the family decide to sell the business.

Archibald McBain from Rothiemurchus purchased the hotel in June 1939 and some of the changes that he made can be seen in this photograph. The name reverted to the Grouse Inn soon after he took over and a drive through in front of the building was constructed which also gave access to a petrol pump. An extension that could cater for coach parties was built shortly after the end of the war. After his death in 1958, the McBain family continued to expand the business and further extensions were added including a lounge, a dance hall and a tea room to cater for coach parties. By the early 1990s there were two tea rooms either side of the original building capable of accommodating up to 200 people at one time while the bar is reputed to offer a choice of 700 different whiskies. Such was the popularity of the Grouse Inn that it was once visited by thirteen coaches on the same day. Visitors can still take lunch in the huge tea room which has on display the handbill advertising the last Ardwell Picnic and Games, but it has been many years since the petrol pump in the driveway served a customer.

Upper Cabrach School    No. 6774

The school in the Upper Cabrach was situated opposite the post office and a short distance from the parish church. The school roll in such an isolated and scattered community was always small and attendance was often erratic. Snowstorms, bad roads and the distance to school were major difficulties. However, distractions such as boys employed in grouse driving while other pupils were away gathering cranberries in the hills were seasonal complaints. It was not surprising that when Banffshire County Council carried out a review of small schools during 1959 it recommended the closure of Upper Cabrach Primary School. The six children on the school roll were transferred to the Lower Cabrach School at Milltown.